18 Things I've Learned

in 18 Years

Zari McFadden

Table of Contents

Introduction

I am an 18-year-old (if you couldn't tell from the title) college student whose mind is constantly churning with ideas and plans, so I wanted to take some of that constant processing and share it with other people. Ever since I was younger, I have always been creative (and a hustler). Whether it was making cardboard bracelets or deserts, I have always been inclined towards creating things, whether they were of value or not. So, in the vein of needing a creative outlet, I decided to share a few of the things that I have learned in my short time on the planet. Now different people with different experiences may have different opinions than I do and that's okay. My experience is not one that encapsulates everyone else's experience and I don't seek to speak for everyone. My goal is to share the things I have learned with hopes of inspiring other people to learn from my experiences and to decide what path they seek to follow in their own lives. I sincerely hope that whoever reads this book finds inspiration and meaningfulness in what I share below. So, I present *18 Things I've Learned in 18 Years...*

1. Don't rush, but don't hold back

We live in a world that is full of opinions. There are opinions about which job you should take, what you should major in, what school you should go to, and so on. Unfortunately, most of these opinions are misinformed and come from people who have no idea of who you are, and what your goals are. Before I get into what I mean by "don't rush, but don't hold back", I want to share a little bit of my story.

I started college at 16 years old. That means that I was, and still am, two years younger than most of my peers. To get to this point, I had to skip a couple of grades. The first grade I technically skipped was 8th grade. I say technically because when I was in 7th grade, I was taking high school math with other advanced students. I went to a Montessori school for my 7th grade year, and my class was a mix of 7th and 8th graders. To take the advanced math class, I had to take classes with the 8th grade students in my class. By the end of the school year, I had already completed the

5

majority of the course work for 8th grade, and I didn't want to redo the same work next year. This led to me asking my parents about graduating middle school early, and they helped me accomplish that goal.

To graduate early, I took a placement test to see if I would even place high enough to be expected to do well in high school. My test scores were high enough to justify graduating early. After that, some of my teachers and my principal sat me down to basically stage an intervention. They gave me their opinions about me graduating early, and gave me some alternative ideas to try to make me change my mind. I entertained the conversation, but I maintained my position because I was strong in what I wanted to do and believed in my own vision at the time.

After it was confirmed that I could graduate with the 8th grade class that year, I finished my year as an 8th grader, with the exception that I still had to take the 7th grade end of grade exams along with the 8th grade science exam, and 9th grade math exam. I did everything I had to do, and I graduated with the 8th graders.

Fast forward two years, and I am a sophomore in high school. One day I was sitting in my Latin class, and I started writing out all the courses I had completed thus far, and the courses that I planned to take in the future, so that I could graduate. As I was doing this, I realized that I would only need to stay for senior year for three classes. To me, this seemed like a waste of a year, so when I got home that afternoon, I told my mom that I wanted to graduate early. I told her that I would only need to stay in school senior year for three classes, and then I told her that I could take those classes online during the summer and during the second semester of my sophomore year. I met with my high school counselor, finding courses I could take online, and planned my next steps.

The second semester of my sophomore year, I took an extra online class. The summer after sophomore year, I took two more online classes. When the next school year started, I had all the credits I needed to be classified a senior. During the first semester of my junior year, I came in as a junior so that I could take the ACT at my school for free, along with the PSAT, but the next semester, I had my status changed to a senior.

During my whole junior/senior year, I was doing the things that I needed to do as a junior along with the things I needed to do as a senior, such as applying for college and scholarships. Throughout that year, a lot of people gave their opinions about whether I should graduate early. A lot of people felt that I was rushing my life away and that I should just stay in school to avoid the responsibilities of adulthood in the future. Of course, there were also a lot of people that supported my decision, but regardless of their opinions, I had to stay strong and hold onto what I thought was best for me.

This leads me to my point of "don't rush, but don't hold back" because I never felt like I was rushing my life away, I just felt like I was moving forward with my next steps in life. My journey is not going to be your journey. Throughout my journey, I learned that moving at a different pace than other people doesn't necessarily mean rushing. It's okay to take a different path at a different time. The key is knowing what works for you, and doing that. Always follow your heart and what you believe is best for you, and the rest will work itself out.

2. Start investing now (money)

Time waits for no one. No matter how much you want it to slow down, time flies and it's up to you to make it work in your best interest. One of the best and easiest ways to make time work for you is through investing. Disclaimer: I am in no way an investing guru or financial advisor, so take the advice that is presented to you with a grain of salt.

Both of my parents are self-employed, so growing up, I was always taught to pursue entrepreneurship and work for myself. When I was younger, I had a lot of hustles. Some of these included selling cardboard bracelets, cakes, cookie batter, scarves, and homemade body care products. As I got older and life got more real, I didn't continue these side hustles because of time constraints and other responsibilities.

During my brief stint as a child entrepreneur, my mom would always make me put at least 10% of whatever money I made in a savings account. At the time, I hated it because as a child you don't think about long term benefits, you think about spending the money that you have in your hand right away. As I've grown older, I've started thinking more about my future and what my long-term goals are. One of these goals is financial independence. One of the easiest ways to set yourself up for financial independence is through long-term investing.

Before I continue, I must emphasize the point of **long-term** investing. Majority of people who invest in stocks for the short term lose money. This is generally because they haven't given their money enough time to grow, or they sell shares as soon as the market starts to drop and end up losing money. In the stock market, time is your best asset because historically the stock market has been on an upwards trend since its inception despite the Great Depression and the 2008 recession.

As a teenager or college student, time is one of your greatest assets, and investing could be a great vehicle for optimizing this asset. Normally at this age you are only responsible for your immediate wants.

You normally don't have any bills to pay because your parents are covering all or most of your expenses. You might be working a job because you want to have money to buy clothes, go out to eat, or hang out with friends. This is the best time to invest. Why? Because you have a high-risk tolerance. Even if you lost all your money in the stock market, it would not be detrimental to you because you have time to bounce back. Compared to a 40-year-old with a family and bills, you have an advantage. You have time for your money to accrue interests and to receive dividends. You have time for companies to grow larger and increase their share prices, so that you can sell your shares for more than you bought them and make a profit.

Let's say you're working a part time job, and you save up $3,000 and decide to invest it in a Vanguard index fund. Since its inception, the VTSMX has had an average 9.54% annual return. So let's say you decide to invest $3,000 in that fund with an average annual return of 9.54%, and you decide not to add any more money to that fund. In ten years, that money would have grown to $7,461.89. In twenty-years, that money would have grown to $18,559.92. Without you doing anything, your money would have doubled or tripled itself. That's the beauty of compound interest in combination with time. When you start to think of money this way, you start to think of ways to make your money work for you instead of you working for money.

Once you change your mindset towards money, and start to think of it as an asset that can work for you, you will start to see how things like time that could work against you, can also work for you. Whatever you want to achieve in life, you can achieve, but you must also have money to survive. Instead of living an unfulfilled life that is focused solely on making money, learn how to invest, so that your money can make you more money, so that you can live the life you want to live instead of the life you have to live to survive.

3. Reward yourself

Life is short. I know that 80, 90, 100 years feels like a long time, but in comparison to how long the Earth and Universe have been around, it's not that long. I say that to say life is too short to not live it to the fullest, and do your best to achieve whatever goals you set for yourself. What comes along with achieving your goals, is rewarding yourself for your achievements. These rewards don't have to be expensive over the top rewards, they can be small things that you promise yourself to motivate you to complete whatever task you have or whatever goal you hope to achieve.

In this world of more than 7 billion people, the only person who is going to accomplish what you want to accomplish, is you. Family and friends might support you and offer guidance, but at the end of the day, it is up to you to achieve your dreams. That means, to achieve success, you must validate your own work and achievements. As supportive as your parents may be, they won't always understand why a certain accomplishment is important to you. Therefore, you must start to reward yourself.

As a college student, there is a lot of stuff going daily. Between classes, homework, clubs, volunteering, internships, research projects, and non-school related hobbies, it is very easy to get burned out and lose focus. To help myself stay motivated, I give myself goals to achieve, and reward myself. For example, if I have a busier than normal week, I motivate myself to get through it by saying that for the weekend I will do nothing but sit in my bed and watch Netflix. I know this may not seem all that rewarding, but when you've reached an exhaustion that has penetrated deeply through your bones, then there is nothing you want to do more than sleep or watch mindless TV.

Other things that I do is set longer-term goals, and give myself bigger gifts once I reach those goals. For example, during the winter break after my first semester of freshman year, I bought myself an iPad Pro and Apple Pencil. Now I won't lie, this was a pretty expensive gift, but I was proud of myself for ending the semester with all A's and I knew that I would use it to take notes in class, read eBook versions of my textbooks, and write on PDF's. I can honestly say that that was one of my best purchases, and it motivated me to perform just as well the next semester.

One of my current goals is to invest in a Vanguard stock index fund. These funds have relatively expensive minimum balances, especially for a college student, but I know that over time, I will make a much higher return on my investment, than if I just spent the same amount of money over a longer period. A few weeks ago, Apple announced the iPhone X, and I know that I want to get it when it comes out. Now I know that this is an expensive phone, so I've told myself that I wouldn't be able to get the iPhone X until I've invested in the stock index fund. Why did I do this? Because if I spent the money for the iPhone X, I would be delaying when I could invest in the index fund, and as I mentioned in a previous chapter, time is money. I also know that whatever return I get on my investment, I could use to pay for the iPhone X, and then I wouldn't really be paying for it out of pocket.

Now I know that these are somewhat extreme examples, and this is because I like high-tech toys, but for you, this can translate to anything. Maybe your vice is shoes is instead of technology. Then set some goals for yourself, and use the pair of shoes that you really want as the incentive for achieving your goal. Maybe you prefer going on vacations. Set some goals for the year, plan your vacation, and go on said vacation as a reward for achieving your goals. Life is too short for all work and no reward. With all that's going on in the world, it is so easy to get burned out and lose motivation. To combat that, set goals and rewards for yourself to help you push forward.

4. Pursue whatever interests you and invest in yourself

In the age of social media, it is easy to feel incompetent. To feel like you're not doing enough with your life, or that what you're doing is less worthy than what other people are doing. Banish any of those thoughts from your mind right now. You are worthy of whatever your goals are, and your interests are just as important as anyone else's. You can't go through life trying to do what everyone else is doing. Everyone on the planet has a purpose, and the purpose of life is to find your purpose, and live it. You can't do that if you're trying to be everyone, but who you are.

Throughout my life, I have had many interests. When I was younger I enjoyed cooking and baking. That led to me selling cakes and desserts to friends and family. As I got older, my interests shifted to making body care products, so I learned how to make whipped Shéa Butter, lotion and deodorant. I sold those products for a while, but then I got bored. I then learned how to make infinity scarves. I did that for about a year, and sold them to my mom's Facebook friends, but once again, I got bored. I decided that I wanted to learn how to make soap - not from one of the soap making kits you get from Michael's, but true soap where you have to mix the lye with the water and oil, and wait a couple of months for the chemical process to take place. The first time I attempted to make soap, it was almost a complete failure. I say almost because I learned what not to do next time, which means that I gained something from the experience.

After my first soap attempt, I wanted to change gears and learn something else, so I decided to learn how to sew. To accomplish this, I would sew my own prom dress. To help me with this task, my mom enlisted the help of a family friend, and in the months leading up to prom, I learned how to sew by sewing my own dress. After I sewed my prom dress, I decided that I would sew my own graduation dress, and that was the project that I worked on the rest of my senior year of high school.

After I graduated, I wanted to try making soap again. Using what I learned from my first soap making attempt, I adjusted the ingredients, and restarted the process at the beginning of the summer. I don't know if any of you have ever made soap from scratch before, but if you haven't, then you should know that it takes between 4 to 6 weeks for homemade soap to be ready for use. I knew that I wanted to be able to use my soap before I started college, so I mixed the ingredients and set up everything at the beginning of summer, let the chemical process take place throughout the summer, and packed it up and took it with me to school at the end of summer. Even though it took a long time for me to reap the rewards for my labor, it was a worthwhile experience because it was the best soap that I had ever used in my life.

I share these stories to show that it's okay to pursue different interests. You don't have to follow one path for the rest of your life. It's okay to not know what you're passionate about. It's okay to want to try everything under the sun. Even now, as a college student, I participate in a wide variety of things. I'm a computer science major who's interested in history, psychology, and social justice. I'm a research assistant on a music project. I'm writing an eBook, while learning about how to invest. The wider your skillset is, the more marketable you become. I know that society tries to fit everybody into a little box, but the truth of the matter is that people are ever evolving. Our interests are ever evolving. Our progression is ever evolving. One of the best things that you can do for yourself is invest in your interests and knowledge. This allows you to broaden your horizons while also saving you from future regret. You miss 100% of the shots you don't take.

5. Waking up early improves productivity

This chapter might sound weird coming from a sleep deprived college student, but in my humble opinion, waking up early is one of the best things that you can do for yourself. For me, early is 5:00 AM. I started waking up at this time to increase my productivity. As a student, once my classes are over for the day, I am normally drained. I don't get as much work done as I need to, so I end up staying up later than I should which leads to me being even more tired the next day. I decided that something had to give. I couldn't stay sleep deprived and unproductive. After watching YouTube videos and researching the benefits of waking up early, I decided to give it a try.

The first morning I did it, I noticed that I got more work done in less time when compared to how much I got done in the afternoon after my classes. I was more motivated to get my work done because I didn't have anything else to do besides work. That morning I was able to work out for a little bit, relish the silence of my dorm, watch the sun rise, and do other things that I had been putting off. Since I was the only one up, I wasn't distracted by outside noises or other things that I could be doing, so I was able to focus on what was right in front of me. Even during the day, I wasn't as tired as I expected to be. I actually felt the opposite of how I would normally feel throughout the day. I wasn't as bone tired, and I was able to get more work done throughout the day.

To wake up early, I had to go to bed early. I am someone who needs a full eight hours of sleep to function at my optimal level, so I had to start going to bed at 9:00 PM. I know that this seems impossible for a college student, but when you get all your work done in the morning before the day begins, then you have the ability and the free time to be able to focus on what you want to focus on, even if that includes going to bed early. I enjoy being able to go to bed without feeling stressed about whether I am going to complete an assignment on time or not.

The best advice that I can give to people who are interested in waking up early, is to go to bed on time. It's not realistic to expect to be able to go to bed at midnight and wake up at 5:00 AM, and still be able to function throughout the day. I would also recommend writing down the reasons why you want to wake up early, and what you hope to achieve by waking up early. I have a list of things that I'm interested in doing or learning that I don't have time to focus on during the day, so I just do it in the morning once I get necessary tasks out the way. It also helps if you wake up immediately after you hear your alarm go off. Don't keep hitting the snooze button, just get up and get moving.

Once you master waking up early, you can begin to master other things. It takes a lot of discipline and self-control to force yourself out of your warm, comfortable bed, and into the cold air to do homework. Once you have been able to suppress and overcome your desire for sleep, you can begin to master the harder aspects of life.

6. The process is more important than the results

"If the path be beautiful, let us not ask where it leads." – Anatole France

In this capitalistic world, very few things matter more than money. Throughout history, the character of people has been compromised for a few dollars. Almost everything today has a price attached to it. This makes the world a dangerous place to live in. This environment is dangerous because people will begin to do anything for a dollar, even if it means stealing, fighting or even killing someone else.

In this kind of world, it's easy to try to forego or ignore the process that it takes to reach success because you don't get rewarded for the process. Your bills aren't getting paid because of the process. Your family isn't eating because of the process. Your bills are getting paid and your family is eating because of the results of the process. Although this may be true, this kind of mentality is dangerous because it can have adverse effects on your health when things don't work out the way you want them to.

For example, say you have a job, and your life is dependent on the money you make on this job. Let's say that you get fired from this job and suddenly you don't have the money to take care of and provide for your family. In that moment, you are stressed and overwhelmed because you have lost your primary means of income. If you only focus on the fact that you don't have a way to achieve your results, then you forget about the skills you have acquired working at your previous job, and you're not thinking about how you can use that skill set to develop a new mean of income or get another job. When you constantly think about the results, you lose sight of the other things that you gain from different experiences.

Why is the process more important than the results? Because through the process of achieving your goal or desired results, you are growing as a person. You are learning new skills and developing your character. Skill sets and character are transferable. They don't rely on a specific place, time, or environment.

For example, say you're an entrepreneur starting an online business. As an entrepreneur, you don't typically see immediate returns on your investments in your business. Oftentimes, you lose money before you make money. Say you decided to quit your job so that you can focus on your online business full time, but after a few months you still haven't made any money, and you're going into debt trying to pay your bills on time. After a few months, you decide that your business has failed and you close your online business. If you only focused on the results of your business, then you would begin to think of yourself as a failure without realizing that you have developed a new skill set that you can use at your next job or use to start another business. If you focused on the process you took to start your online business, then you could look at what you did wrong, come up with a new plan of action, and achieve more success in the future.

In a society that's all about the bottom line, it's easy to forget the journey you take to become who you are, and only worry about the results. This mindset of only caring about results can be dangerous because it can lead to disappointment and dissatisfaction. Disappointment and dissatisfaction are factors that can decline your mental health, which in turn can affect your physical health. Once you learn to value the process more than the results, then you can start to receive joy out of life regardless of the results that you get, which can contribute to future success and better mental health.

7. Have Multiple Streams of Income

Early in this book I stated that both of my parents are self-employed. My dad is a bails-bondsman with a Real Estate license, and my mom is a Real Estate Agent and a Travel Agent. What I've learned from being around my parents is the importance of having multiple streams of income. As a Real Estate Agent and Travel Agent, my mom goes to a lot of different conferences, watches different webinars, and participates in various conference calls to help better herself in her specific areas. A common theme that is present throughout these sessions is the importance of having multiple streams of income.

Unfortunately, the vast majority of people only have one source of income, and that is their primary job. This is dangerous because it doesn't allow for flexibility or financial security. When you rely solely on one source of income, you lose your ability to support yourself if you lose your job. With only one source of income, you also limit your income

29

potential. The amount of money you can make is limited to the number of hours you can work. With this kind of system, you will never be able to achieve financial independence because you have to work for money instead of allowing money to work for you.

Now coming up with multiple streams of income doesn't have to be a hard task. One way to start could be to invest in a stock index fund or Real Estate Investment Trust (REITS). Both of these investment types have high rates of returns and dividend yields. The Vanguard Total Stock Market Index Fund (VTSAX) has had an average 7.11% rate of return over the past ten years. This is a much higher rate than you would get by solely keeping money in a savings account of CD (certificate of deposit).

REITs on the other hand are investment vehicles that allow you to invest in different sectors of the Real Estate market. These types of investments have higher dividend yields than most other stocks because they have to pay out at least 90% of their revenue to investors as dividends. This a great investment if you're someone who is interested in investing in the Real Estate market, but don't have enough capital to buy a house outright. REITs are also great because they tend to be less volatile than other companies, so you get a consistent return on investment.

Some other examples of streams of income you can have are a part time job, an eBook, a YouTube channel that you have monetized, or an online blog with advertisements and affiliate links. A part time job is a great stream of income if you need guaranteed money, but you only have a short amount of time. An eBook is another great way to generate a stream of income. You can create one for little to no cost, sell across different platforms, and use it as a tool to develop a customer base for other products or businesses that you hope to develop in the future. A YouTube channel is another great option, but it can take time to build a following and make significant money. You also may have to invest in recording equipment before you start. Lastly, another possible stream of income is an online blog. This is also something that can take time to build up and start generating income, but it is also something that you can start part time, and continue to build.

As you can see, there are a lot of different options, listed and unlisted, for creating multiple streams of income. When you create multiple streams of income, you give yourself financial security, and start to increase your financial independence. I am currently in the process of developing my multiple streams of income. I have invested in REITs and other stocks, life insurance with cash value, and I am in the process of publishing an eBook and investing in a stock index fund. As previously stated, one of my ultimate goals in life is to achieve financial independence, so I am trying to capitalize on my young age and status as a student to help me do this. Life is meant to be lived to the fullest, not held back by financial liabilities and responsibilities.

8. Stress decreases health - learn healthy coping mechanisms

As I am writing this book, I am taking a Psychology course at my school. Even though I am a Computer Science major and Psychology has little to do with programming, this class has easily become one of my most impactful courses. The reason why I love this course so much, is because it has so much to do with my existence as a human being, and helps me better understand myself. One of the things that we have been talking about a lot in this class, is the effects of stress on the body and on your health. Learning about this has inspired me to make more conscientious choices about what I allow to have impact on my life because I don't want to be negatively impacted by avoidable stress.

Before I go into details about some healthy coping mechanisms for dealing with stress, I want to talk about why stress has such an impact on health in the first place. A lot of people have heard of the fight-

or-flight response, but may not understand the full implications of this response. When a person becomes triggered by a stressor, your body activates its fight-or-flight response. When this response is activated, your body shuts down all non-essential functions like your immune system and reproductive system, and pours all its available energy and resources to other parts of your body like your heart, lungs, and muscles. This is why your heart rate increases along with your breathing. This is also why people have adrenaline rushes that allow them to access a strength that they don't normally have access to. For example, a mother might lift a car off her trapped child.

This fight-or-flight response is great when you are in actual danger and need to save yourself, but it's not so great for things that aren't physically harmful. Unfortunately, many of the stressors that humans face today, are mental stresses that we place on ourselves. Things like stressing about paying bills, being stuck in traffic, or disagreements amongst friends can trigger this response. This is dangerous because it means that our bodies are constantly in the state of fight-or-flight which means that non-essential systems are constantly suppressed and other things like blood pressure are constantly high. These systems constantly being on means that your risk of heart disease, stroke, and cancer are higher because your body is unable to fight off the things that make you sick. Of course there are a lot of other factors that are present when your body is under stress, but this just goes to show some of the reasons why constant stress is dangerous for your health.

Now that you understand the implications of being stressed, let's talk about some ways to help cope with stress. In Psychology, the two main forms of coping are problem-focused coping, and emotion focused coping. Problem-focused coping involves decreasing or eliminating the problem that is causing stress. For example, if a student is stressed about an exam, to help eliminate that stress, they could study the material necessary for the exam, and build their confidence. Emotion-focused coping on the other hand involves improving your emotional response to the stressor. For example, the same student instead of studying for the exam may decide to eat ice cream and watch Netflix to deal with the emotional impact of the stress. Emotion-focused coping is great for controlling your response to things you can't control. For example, if you are at higher risk of developing cancer, you can't really do anything to change your risk, but you can control your emotional response to the risk.

Both coping mechanisms are great, but there are other things that you can also do to help with stress. For example, practicing yoga and meditation is great for dealing with stress because it forces you to be fully present in the moment, and not think about all the things you have to do. This is great because it allows your body to reset itself, and for you to refocus your energy and mentally prepare for the things you must do. Another approach that you can use to handle stress is to write down all of your fears, the worst outcomes of your fears, and how you would handle those outcomes. This method is great because it gives you a plan of action for dealing with different stressors.

Stress is an unavoidable part of life because it helps humans survive and progress. Without stress, there would be no motivation to get things done and move forward. Stress only becomes a negative when it becomes a consistent part of your life and puts undue pressure on your body, affecting your health. The only way to lessen the impact of stress on your body, is to take control of the things that are stressing you out, or to change your emotional response to the stressor. Don't allow things that are within your control and out of your control to impact your health and life expectancy.

9. Believe in yourself, you control your destiny

In this age of information and technology, it's easy to feel like there are so many factors in life that are out of your control. To a certain extent this is true. For example, you have little control over who becomes president, what legislation is passed, how much money you pay for taxes or climate change. However, you do have control over yourself and your abilities. You can control the people you hang out with, the amount of money you spend, what you devote time and energy to, and how you treat other people. These are the things that determine what kind of future you will have.

It's not about where you're from, it's about where you're going. I know that almost everybody has heard some variation of that statement at some point in their lives. This is an honest statement. You can't control the environment that you grew up in, but you can control the environment you will be placed in in the future. For example, a lot of people have grown up in "the hood" with little resources. As a child, you can't control that, but you can control your ability to get out. You can make a conscious effort to make straight A's in school, get a scholarship to college, and get out of that environment. Or you can choose to sell drugs, do bad in school, and become a victim of the school-to-prison pipeline. Sure, it's not your fault that systems have been put into place to make certain aspects of life harder for some people than they are for others, but it is up to you whether or not you fall victim to those systems.

Another example of this can be found in the fact that we live in a capitalistic society that benefits off the backs of the working class. It's out of your control the fact that this is the society we live in. It's out of your control that this system has put barriers in the way of people achieving success. What is in your control however, is the ability to find ways to overcome these obstacles. I'm not saying that it won't be hard or challenging because it will. A person will always be a victim if they make themselves a victim.

You can fall victim to childhood abuse and neglect, but it's up to you whether you allow those experiences to control your future. You can fall victim to drug and alcohol abuse, but it's up to you whether you stay a victim. Life was not meant to be easy. You are meant to experience trials and tribulations so that you can continue to grow and reach your full potential. If you are constantly focusing on all the things that have gone wrong in your life, all the people that have hurt you, or all the things that you have done to hurt other people, then you will be stuck in a constant cycle. It is necessary to learn how to pick yourself up from all the negative experiences that have impacted your life and keep going.

One of the trials that I have experienced in my life has been having seizures. When I was 12 years old, I had a seizure in the middle of the night. I was sleeping on the top bunk in the room that I shared with my sister when my mom heard my foot banging against the wall. Both of my parents then came to my room, got me off the top bunk, and called 911. When the emergency dispatchers got to my house they did a neurological check on me, and determined that I was good to stay home since my seizure stopped. They left, but not too long after, I had another seizure. This time, I was taken to the hospital and they did some tests and scans to try to figure out what was causing the seizures. There was nothing on my brain scans, so the doctors just said that sometimes children have seizures, but then grow out of them.

After that we left the hospital, and my parents decided to take me to see a holistic doctor to figure out what was going on. That doctor determined that eating added sugar was causing spikes in my brain activity leading to seizures, and said that I needed to stop eating sugar if I didn't want to have any more seizures. Of course, I stopped eating added sugar along with other high glycemic index foods, but it was not an easy thing to do. All my favorite food and drinks had some form of added sugar, but I had to decide that my health was more important than my desire for sugar. To this day, I still cannot eat foods with high sugar contents, but I've learned to adjust with what I can eat, and have come to appreciate how much healthier it is to not eat sugar.

This was just one example of a trial that I've experienced and have had to grow from because I chose not to allow myself to become a victim to what sugar does to my body. If I had made a different decision, then I would not be able to live life the same way I do now. I say all of this to say that it's up to you who you become. You may not be able to control all the things that happen in your life, but you are able to control your responses to those things. At the end of the day, life is what you make it because you control your destiny.

10. No, you're not too young

Okay, so you might be too young in the eyes of car rental companies to rent a car, but that's not the point. I mentioned earlier in this book that I graduated high school and started college at 16. Even as I write this book, I am only 17 years old. Throughout my life, I've had a lot of people tell me that I am too young or that I am rushing my life. They've told me that I am so mature for my age, and that they weren't as driven as I am at my age. Now all of these things aren't bad, but they show that people place more value on age rather than experience or drive. Even though the saying "age is just a number" is passed around a lot, most people still consider age one of your most defining factors. Well, I want to dispel this myth. Age is not the most defining factor of your life. Age does not determine your personality, ambition, or future success. The only things age tells you about a person is how long they've existed on Earth. That's it.

I am a strong believer that you can do anything

you set your mind to. I believe that success isn't dependent on age, but instead on dedication and time committed. If you want to graduate high school early, then you can. You don't have to take four years to complete high school, you just need have all the credits necessary to graduate. If you want to retire by the age of 30, then you can. You don't have to spend 40+ years working a job you hate, you just must learn how to save and budget your money. If you want to start a nonprofit at 15 or 16, then you can. You just need to have an adult help you with the paperwork, and gather all the information you can before you start.

Unfortunately, society doesn't believe the same things that I believe about age. For example, you must be at least 18 to open a brokerage account, and start investing. To me, this is stupid because a lot of people over the age of 18 make just as many dumb decisions about money as people under the age of 18 because age has nothing to do with financial literacy. However, despite my views about this, I still had to have my mom open my brokerage account in her name because I am not yet 18. On the same note, I won't be able to have my own credit card until I am 18 either, but I am able to have a debit card which has allowed me to develop good spending habits. Unfortunately, the good spending habits I have developed won't allow me to build credit yet, but when I am finally able to start, I won't have a huge learning curve.

Despite what the media says it's okay to think about and prepare for the things that most people don't think about or prepare for until they are in their thirties. If you start thinking about and preparing for the things that you're supposedly too young to care about, then you won't have to be one of the those people that spend majority of their thirties making up for the bad decisions they made in their twenties. It's interesting to me how many people say a teenager is too young to worry about adult things, but then in the same breath, talk about the things they wish they would have done or prepared for in their teens and early twenties. The only way to live a life with no regret is to learn from the mistakes of other people, and heed the advice of people that have already been in your shoes. I don't want to make the same mistakes that so many adults are making or have made, so I aim to do things different, even if I am technically "too young" to worry about these things. You can't move forward if you are constantly reliving history.

11. Live in the present, but prepare
for the future

In this age of information, so many people live their life by the motto: "You Only Live Once" (YOLO). While this statement is true, it's also dangerous because it causes people to make stupid decisions that negatively impact the rest of their lives for the sole reason that "you only live once". People start jumping off buildings, destroying their credit, and spending a check because they'll "get it right back" under the guise of YOLO. These things are not smart decisions. They're not smart decisions because they mean that you'll spend a lot of time in your life trying to make up for them, which means you won't be able to live life to the fullest.

If you decide as a college student that you're going to get a credit card, spend your entire balance buying things you can't afford, and then decide not to pay at least the minimum balance, then you have destroyed your credit, and it can take years to restore that. In the meantime you won't be able to take out a mortgage, you'll have to pay ridiculously high interest on a car you can't afford, and you will be in this cycle of debt that is going to be very hard to get out of.

If you decide that you're going to spend your entire check on frivolous things that you don't need, and that lose value as soon as you buy them because you know that you're going to get paid in two weeks, then you have played yourself. Why? Because you don't get back money that you have already spent. Once you have spent the money, it doesn't come back, you just work more hours to get more money. This is how people start living paycheck to paycheck. At the end of the day, it's not about how much you make, it's about how much you keep.

When I say, "live in the present, but prepare for the future", I don't mean do the things mentioned above. I mean live the present moment fully by doing things you genuinely love, and improving yourself. Physical items don't bring true joy. Sure, buying a new iPhone gives you temporary happiness, but after a while, it'll just be another phone. In this world of materialism, it's easy to get caught up in seeking out items for temporary pleasure, but those things are just that, temporary. True joy comes from knowing your purpose and helping other people. True joy comes from doing things that you genuinely care about. True joy does not come from material items.

On this same note though, it is also important to prepare for the future. When preparing for the future, you should outline your lifetime goals. These may change as you get older, but it's important to have an idea of what you're working for. For me, one of my goals is to achieve financial independence and retire before I'm thirty. Everything that I do up until that point is to help me achieve that goal. Once I reach that goal, I will need to outline some new goals, so that I am constantly motivated to do more.

Although the future may seem far away, time waits for no one. Don't waste precious time on regrets and mistakes. Spend the time you do have doing things that are meaningful to you, and work on achieving your goals. While you're young, work on setting yourself up for future success. Don't set yourself up to spend majority of your adult life and active years working a 9 to 5, and living paycheck to paycheck. Start to make good habits now, so that when you do become an adult, you don't make the same mistakes that other people have made, and continue to make. You can live the life that you want to live, it just takes good judgement and decision making.

12. It's okay to be different

The great thing about being who you are, is that there is no one else like you on the planet. That being said, don't try to make yourself into someone you're not. As Dave Ramsey says, if you want to live like no one else, then you have to live like no one else. You have to diverge away from the bad habits of the people around you, and start to do the things that no one else is doing. You are only as good as the people you keep around you. Your network, is your net worth. Therefore, if you want to have a certain lifestyle, you need to find people who are living like you want to live. You probably shouldn't follow the pack if the whole pack is starving and broke.

You know when you were younger and your mom asked you "if your friends jump off a bridge are you going to jump off a bridge with them" when you did something stupid? Well you need to apply that concept to your life. If all of your friends are miserable, and living paycheck-to-paycheck, are you going to start being miserable, and living paycheck-to-paycheck? If all of your friends are in debt and on the verge of going bankrupt, are you going to go bankrupt with them? Or are you going to decide to live within your means and save up as much money as you can? Are you going to choose to pay a little more to invest in yourself, or just throw that money away on frivolous items like your friends? Are you going to party away a weekend, or use that time to learn a new skill?

Now, I'm not saying not to ever have fun or spend time with friends and family, but I am saying that you should do everything in moderation. If you want to live the same life that your friends are living, then go ahead and follow their lead. If not, then you have to make the decision to do things differently. I know that it's uncomfortable to be different from other people. I know that it's hard to not follow the pack, but to grow, you have to get out of your comfort zone. To make progress, you have to do the thing that other people think is crazy. The road to success is long and requires sacrifices, but the end results are worth it.

An example of this for me was when I was starting school. I started kindergarten when I was 4 years old, but my parents didn't like the school I was in, so they took me out in the middle of the year. The next year they asked me if I wanted to go on to first grade or redo kindergarten. All my friends were going to kindergarten, so of course I decided to start kindergarten again to be with them. That ended up being one of my least favorite decisions I ever made because I ended up holding back my true potential. Of course, later on I ended up skipping two grades anyway, but I probably wouldn't have had to do all the things I did to skip those two grades if I had gone straight to first grade instead of going to kindergarten again.

The reason that I chose to go back to kindergarten wasn't a truly valid reason. Friends or family shouldn't be the reason why you hold yourself back. At the end of the day, it's your life. Moving forward in life doesn't mean that you're leaving people behind, it just means that you are at two different stages. You can still hang out with your same

53

friends outside of school and work, but individuals shouldn't stop you from achieving maximum potential. Don't ever hold yourself back because of what other people think and believe. It's up to you to do what you believe is best for yourself and your future. In the end, you're the one that must live with your decisions, not other people.

13. Self-analysis is necessary for growth

One of the most important things that I've learned, is that self-analysis is important and necessary if you want to grow. If you don't know who you are as an individual, or the flaws you possess, then you are unable to grow and change. You can't fix what you don't know is broken. You can't change what you don't know needs to be changed. The only way to find out what you need to adjust, is to look inside yourself, and find the areas of weakness inside of you. Then you need to figure out the implications of those areas of weakness. Once you figure those things out, then you can make the necessary adjustments to fix those areas.

For example, one of my biggest areas of weakness is a lack of patience. I am someone that is constantly moving forward without pausing. I like to see immediate results, and I get frustrated when things don't work out the way I want them to. I hate working in groups because it takes so much longer to complete assignments. I get annoyed when people don't see the value of something as fast as I do. I am also prone to quitting new ideas if they don't take off the way I want them to. When I was younger, I used to sell skin care products. I stopped selling those products because I wasn't getting my desired results fast enough. As I've gotten older, I've come to the realize that good things take time.

To help myself develop more patience, I've put myself in environments that require patience. For example, I volunteer at an elementary school. Dealing with children takes a lot of self-control and patience because they don't understand concepts the same way that adults do. They don't really understand why they shouldn't run in the hallway, or why it's not nice to push a classmate, so you must be patient when it comes to explaining these ideas to them. I've also tried to develop my patience by approaching things that take time with a better attitude. For example, I want to start a blog soon, but I know that it takes time to see traffic and income from a blog. To prepare myself for this, I've been mentally training myself for this journey.

As you can see, self-analysis for me is important because it has helped me identify factors within myself that may limit my ability to reach success. If I don't master having patience with other people, then I won't have the patience to wait on the good things that are to come in my life. If I just quit when things take too long, then I will miss out on a wide variety of opportunities and possible accomplishments. This is one of the things that I need to improve on as an example, but what you need to work on may be completely different from what I need to work on. Maybe you have patience mastered, but need to better your communication skills, or increase your productivity. The only way for you to know what you need to work on, is to look within yourself, look at past trials and tribulations, and figure out what areas you were weak in, and how you can improve those areas. To grow, you must struggle especially against yourself.

14. Speak things into existence

As you can probably tell by now, I am a strong proponent of believing in yourself and your own abilities. One thing that comes along with that, is the ability of speaking things into existence. When you speak things into existence, you are calling on forces within the universe to conspire in your favor. You are telling the world that what you want to happen, will happen. This means that you truly believe in what you want and in your goals. Faith without works is dead, but work without faith is also dead. How can something you truly want be brought into your life if you don't really believe in it? I don't believe in coincidences or things happening by chance. I believe that good things happen to good people, and that anyone can achieve their goals.

Disclaimer: this doesn't mean that you don't have to put in work or effort to achieve your goals. This means that if you put in the work to reach your goals, the atmosphere and universe will work alongside you to bring whatever goals you have into fruition. No matter how impossible or large your goal may seem, if you believe in it strongly enough, and put the work into it, then it will happen. This doesn't mean that it will happen right away. It doesn't mean that you say you want something, and poof, there it is. It may take years for you to achieve whatever your goal is, but the point is that you will achieve your goal eventually.

A personal example that I have of this can be found in my ability to graduate early. Years before I even started high school, there was a girl that used to babysit my siblings and me. One night while she was babysitting us for my parents, she was telling me about her college experience, and all the different traveling experiences she had. I remember being so amazed at all of the things that she was doing because she had also started college at 16. I remember wanting to have some of the same experiences as her, so that night, I said that I was going to graduate high school, and start college at 16. Now this was way before I was even in high school, I think I may have been in 5th or 6th grade.

When I finally got to high school, I completely forgot about saying that I wanted to graduate early, so my freshman year, I hadn't done anything extra to give myself the ability to graduate early. It wasn't until the end of my junior/senior year of high school that I remembered saying that I was going to graduate at 16. Even though I completely forgot I set that goal, when I originally spoke the thought into existence, I believed so strongly in myself that the universe worked in my favor to help me achieve my goal.

I share that story to say that you can do anything that you set your mind to. It doesn't matter how old you are, how much experience you have, how much money you have, anything that you want for yourself, you can do. When I originally said that I was going to go to college at 16, I didn't even completely understand what college was. I didn't even really understand what high school was, but I was so inspired by what my babysitter was doing, that I knew that I could follow in her footsteps.

The mind is such a powerful tool, and everything you believe about yourself either consciously or subconsciously works its way into your life. If you believe that you are strong, ambitious and worthy of achieving any of the goals you set for yourself, then you will encourage the universe to work for you, and you will subconsciously work for yourself. On the other hand, if you believe that you aren't worthy of achieving your goals, that you are too weak, or that you lack the ability to get what you want out of life, then you will set yourself up for failure.

With these things in mind, I encourage you to speak the things you want into existence right now. I encourage you to write down your goals, and then come up with an action plan to achieve your goals. If you must learn a new skill before you can achieve a goal, then register for a class and learn that skill. If you must build up your self-confidence before you believe in yourself enough to even achieve the goal in the first place, then start to work on building up your confidence. Only you can control your actions and only you are responsible for your future, so believe in yourself because you control your destiny.

15. Gratitude can determine how happy you are with life

Over the past few months, I have been watching a lot of YouTube videos, following blogs, and reading books by relatively successful people. I say relatively because success looks different to each person, but pretty much all of the people I've been following are at a point in their life that I hope to reach eventually. A common theme that I have heard from each of these people is that your level of happiness is not based on how much stuff you have, but rather based on how grateful and appreciative you are of the life you are currently living. Throughout my life, gratitude has been something that has been constantly emphasized, and I try to remain grateful and appreciative of the things that I have. I try to avoid taking for granted the life I live because I understand that there is always somewhere worse you can be in life. Now I don't know if you are a religious person or not, but I have always been taught that God hates ingratitude. Ingratitude is one of the worst sins in life. Whether you believe that or not is up to you.

I have been taught by Minister Farrakhan that one of the consequences of ingratitude is depression. Once again, whether you believe that or not is up to you. I recently listened to the audiobook version of *The 4-Hour Work Week* by Tim Ferriss, and one of the things that he talks about is how depressed he used to be. One of the things that helped him get out of this depression was journaling and writing down the things that he's grateful for. He even recommends the 5 Minute Journal which prompts you to write down three things you're grateful for each day to improve happiness.

Outside of reading about the experiences of other people, the power of gratitude was also emphasized in my yoga class at school. One class period, all we did was have everyone go around the room and say what they were grateful for. From that experience alone, I could see just how impactful it was for everyone to just talk about their life experiences, and giving gratitude for the things that they do have instead of focusing on whatever trial they may have been going through at that point in their life.

Thought is one of the most powerful forms of energy on the planet. Your thoughts determine your actions and your actions determine your quality of life. If you constantly think and believe negative thoughts, then your life will reflect that negativity. If you constantly think and believe positive thoughts, then your life will reflect that positivity. This doesn't mean that you will never go through terrible trials and tribulations, it just means that you will be better able to overcome those trials and grow as a person.

If you ever feel like your life is spinning out of control or that it seems like the universe is working against you, just take a moment to write down the things that you're grateful for. Once you are able to think of the glass as half full instead of half empty, you will then be able to approach problems with a positive attitude and conquer any challenge that is in your way. Nobody ever said that life was meant to be easy. It's a constant journey that is going to test who you are as a person. It will try you in ways that you never expect, you just have to be able to face those challenges head on and learn as much as you can from them. Remember, you are the author of your own fate. You can will into existence whatever you desire as long as you put forth the right amount of effort. Nothing will be handed to you. You have to take the necessary actions to achieve your goals and then allow the universe, God, whatever you believe in, to do the rest. As one of my mentors likes to say, "Everything begins and ends with you".

16. Give and you shall receive

One of the principles that I have been raised on throughout my life is charity. According to Merriam-Webster, charity is *generosity and helpfulness especially toward the needy or suffering; aid given to those in need.* This is an important principle because I believe in the law of reciprocity and that what goes around comes back around. Charity means that you sacrifice something of yourself whether that's time, money or energy, for the good of someone else. Charity means that you give out of what's given to you, and it's related to gratitude. If you feel fulfilled in life, and you are grateful for what you have, then you should feel honored to give part of what you have to other people, and spread the joy that you have in your life.

One of the most common themes that I have heard throughout my study of whom I deem to be successful individuals, is that they all make it a point to give back to their community in the form of charity.

For some people this means donating to their church, for others it means starting foundations that give scholarships to students in low income communities. Sometimes it means starting a mentoring program to help troubled youth. Other times it means donating to other causes such as feeding the homeless, or helping those that have been hurt by natural disasters. Acts of charity look different to each individual, but they all have the common theme of giving out of what you have been given.

In *Money: Master the Game* by Tony Robbins, Robbins talks about how your wealth is associated with the number of people you serve. The more people you serve, the wealthier you are. The definition of wealth is different for each person. For some people, wealth may mean money. For others it may mean relationships, or a having a strong spiritual connection to a higher power. An example of what this looks like can be found by looking at the richest people in the world money wise. The richest man in the world right now is Jeff Bezos, the founder of Amazon. His net worth right now is $98.8 Billion. Yes, that is billion with a B. Right now, there are approximately 80 million Amazon Prime users. That means that Jeff Bezos company is serving at least 80 million people. However, this doesn't include the number of people that use Amazon who aren't prime members. This also doesn't include the number of people who shop at places like Zappos, Whole Foods, and other companies that Amazon owns. As you can see, Amazon is serving a lot of people around the world, and that is why Jeff Bezos is the richest man in the world right now. The same can be said for Bill Gates (Microsoft), Mark Zuckerberg (Facebook), Amancio Ortega (Zara), Warren Buffett (Berkshire Hathaway), etc.

No matter how you personally may feel about the richest people in the world, you have to recognize that each of these people built a product that improves the lives of other people, and have been able to exponentially increase the number of people their product serves. This idea of increasing the amount of people you serve to increase your wealth is not a new idea. It's not anything spooky or evil. It's about using your own talents and creativity to solve a problem. That's the secret to wealth. The caveat to this however, is to not give to other people with the expectation of getting it back in return. You have to be genuine in whatever way you serve people.

Everything that I have talked about here, I believe wholeheartedly, and I try to consistently be a charitable person, whether that means giving my time in mentoring elementary to high school students, or donating money to causes that I genuinely believe in. And from my own experience, I have never given anything away that I have not gotten back tenfold. Just remember, whatever you do, in good or evil, will come back around to you or to your family.

17. It's not about how much you make, it's about how much you keep

Something that I have consistently talked about throughout this book has been finances and wealth building. I have been constantly bringing these things up because I have been doing a lot of research about how I can set myself up to be in a position of financial security way before the age of 65. The most common piece of advice that I have heard is that it's not about how much you make, but rather how much you keep. I have seen a lot of videos that compare the salary of a doctor to that of a plumber, but show how in the end, the plumber ends up ahead because of the way he saves and invests his money. The idea behind these videos is to show that wealth isn't necessarily dependent upon how much money you make a year, but rather on how much of that money you save and invest. There is someone in every income bracket that is living paycheck to paycheck. From doctors and lawyers to janitors and teachers. Each of these fields have vastly different income ranges, but that means nothing if the individual spends all their money. Sure, the type of life each individual has may be different, but the quality of life is not much different if everyone is worried about paying their bills next month.

We live in a society that is driven by consumerism and materialism. Everybody wants the newest toy or gadget or fashion item, but these things will leave you broke. Now, I am not picking on anybody or trying to call anyone out because I am someone who likes to have nice things, but I have recognized that consistently buying new and unnecessary items will not lead to increased happiness, and may eventually lead to financial slavery. I have decided that financial freedom is more important to me than material possessions. Don't get me wrong, I'm not holding myself back from buying things that I really want, I just wait a minute before I get them to make sure it's not an impulsive purchase. In addition, I also make sure that I pay myself first with any money I get. That means that before I buy anything new, I make sure I have saved and invested a part of my money. By doing this, I am allowing myself to get the things that I really want, while also setting myself up to be financially free in the future because my investments will allow my money to make me more money and compound over time.

As a college student, I know how easy it is to spend unnecessary money. A few dollars for a snack here, a few more dollars for a shirt there, and before you know it, you've spent $100 that you didn't really have to spend. This is even worse for new graduates who have gotten their first real adult job with real adult money. Trust me, it's easy to go splurge on a shopping trip when you see your bank account after your direct deposit hits. These "little" impulse buys are why it's important to save and invest first and spend last. Something that I plan to set up before my internship this summer, is a Roth IRA. If I could, I would also try to open a Roth 401K. Why am I thinking about these things while I'm a student? I am thinking about these things now because I want to get myself in the mind of being an investor before I graduate into the real world. I want to set myself up to be disciplined enough to go ahead and start investing as much money as I can before I have real bills or a family to take care of. In this day and age, only saving 5% of your check is not going to be enough to retire on. I have plans to reach retirement savings by the time I'm 30. I can't do this if I don't start disciplining myself now. I have it in my mind right now that as soon as I get a job, I will max out my Roth IRA and Roth 401K.

Quick Side Note: A Roth IRA is an investment vehicle that allows you to invest up to $5,500 a year in taxed income as long as you reach certain requirements. What this means for you is that any income you make from compound interest, is yours tax free when you withdraw it. Now there are certain stipulations about withdrawals that you can learn about later, but for now, just understand that this is a great tool because you don't know what future taxes may be, so you'll be secure in whatever money you earn over time. A Roth 401K is like a regular 401K, but instead of your money being tax deferred until withdrawal, you pay taxes on your money upfront, and never pay taxes again on any money you've earned overtime. The current max that you can contribute to a

Roth 401K is $18,000 a year if you are under 50 years old. You can contribute $24,000 if you are over the age of 50.

Both investment vehicles are great tools to help you in your path to building wealth, and they give you the freedom of mind from worrying about future taxes on earnings, especially if you think your tax bracket will increase in the future.

Once you make the decision that you will not be a slave to financial stress, it is up to you to take the steps necessary to buy your freedom. Financial freedom looks different for everyone, so it's up to you to decide what it looks like to you personally. Two books that I highly recommend to get started is *Rich Dad Poor Dad* by Robert Kiyosaki and *Money: Master the Game* by Tony Robbins. Both books give different perspectives on money and wealth, and will start you in the right path to achieving your financial goals. Just remember that the first rule of money is that it's not about how much you make, it's about how much you keep.

18. I hate working out, but the benefits are real

The last thing that I want to cover in this book, is physical health and wellness. I have talked about money a lot in this book because it is an important aspect of everybody's life no matter where you're from, but another important aspect of life is physical wellbeing. You can only do as much as your body can do. Sure, you may have spontaneous moments of strength and endurance, especially if you are in a life or death situation, but these spontaneous moments won't last forever. In order to have a better quality of life, you must take care of both your mind and body.

As you can probably tell from the title of this section, I am someone who has a love hate relationship with working out. It's not that I doubt the benefits of working out, I just hate most of the workout things I do. I hate going to the gym and working out in front of a lot of people. I'm not really into sports even though I grew up playing soccer at the

YMCA. As my dad says, I am more left-brained than right-brained meaning I am into logic and analysis. I would rather spend time writing a computer program, than I would playing a game outside. This has led to me being the least in shape person in my household. Pretty much everybody in my house does some regular fitness activity. My sister plays basketball, my brother boxes, my dad goes to the same gym as my brother, and my mom runs on the treadmill every morning, and me, well I just avoided any physical activity until recently.

One of the graduation requirements for my school is that we have to take at least two wellness classes. I decided this past semester to just get my two wellness classes out the way, and ended up taking strength training and yoga. Over the past semester, I have fallen in love with yoga. I love that there's no expectations in class. Each pose challenges you in one way or another, but you can make modifications based on your body. I also love that the focus is more on breathing and building a spiritual connection than on how long you can hold a pose. When I leave a yoga class, I feel more connected and relaxed than I did when I entered the class originally. I also feel like I am doing significant work on my body because yogis are some of the strongest people have I ever seen in my life. The body strength that someone who has practiced yoga for years has is so amazing, and what they can do with their bodies is something that I see as an achievable goal for myself.

Since I have found an exercise type that I enjoy doing, and do on a consistent basis, I have noticed improvements in my body. I have always been a pretty healthy person because I have a strict diet that I've been following since birth, but physical activity was always the area I lacked in. Now that I have found something I enjoy doing, I have noticed that my body is stronger and my flexibility has improved. If I work out in the morning, then I notice I have more energy throughout the day. If I work out at night, then I notice that I get better sleep at night. I also have noticed that I feel more focused and at peace with myself. When I practice yoga, I generally go by myself, so besides getting the physical activity, I also use it as a form of self-care because I use that time to focus on myself. I believe that everyone should take time to be by themselves and to enjoy their own company, so I use my time in yoga to do that. Yoga has become something that I am excited to do and I try to share my excitement with other people.

So as someone who used to hate exercising, I encourage everyone to go out and find some physical activity that you enjoy doing. Whether it's yoga, basketball, boxing or Pilates, make sure that you are getting physically active. It's not enough to just eat healthy, you also must physically push your body. Not only is it great for your physical health and wellbeing, it's also great for your mental health and wellbeing. So, go forth and be active.

Conclusion

No matter where you're at in your life, you will constantly be bombarded with opinions. Opinions about who you are. Opinions about who you should be. Opinions about where you should be in life at certain ages and opinions about imaginary milestones you should be aiming to achieve. Whether you subscribe to these opinions or not is completely up to you. We only have a limited amount of time on the planet, so it's up to us to determine how we want to spend this time. Since my time on the planet thus far has been relatively short, I still have a lot of learning and maturing to do. I fully expect for my thoughts on certain matters to change over time, I don't expect my 28-year-old self to think the same as my 18-year-old self. With that said, I hope that you have enjoyed learning about 18 Things I've Learned in 18 Years and I hope that you take some of the things that I've learned in my own life and apply them to your life.

With Love,

Zari

CPSIA information can be obtained
at www.ICGtesting.com
Printed in the USA
LVHW091959100419
613688LV00001B/2/P

9 780578 485300